LISTEN to the WIND

THE STORY of DR. GREG and *THREE CUPS OF TEA*

BY Greg Mortenson AND Susan L. Roth

COLLAGES BY Susan L. Roth

Dial Books for Young Readers

For Julia and for Leo, with love—S.L.R.

In Memory of Haji Ali—G.M., S.L.R.

We are the children of
Korphe. We live in a village
in the mountains of Pakistan.
Our families grow and gather
the food we eat. Our mothers
weave and sew the clothes we
wear. We make up our games,
and we make our own toys.
We read our books, and
we write with our pencils.
We study in the school that
we helped to build.

Before our school was built,
we had lessons outside.
We wrote with sticks,
on the ground.

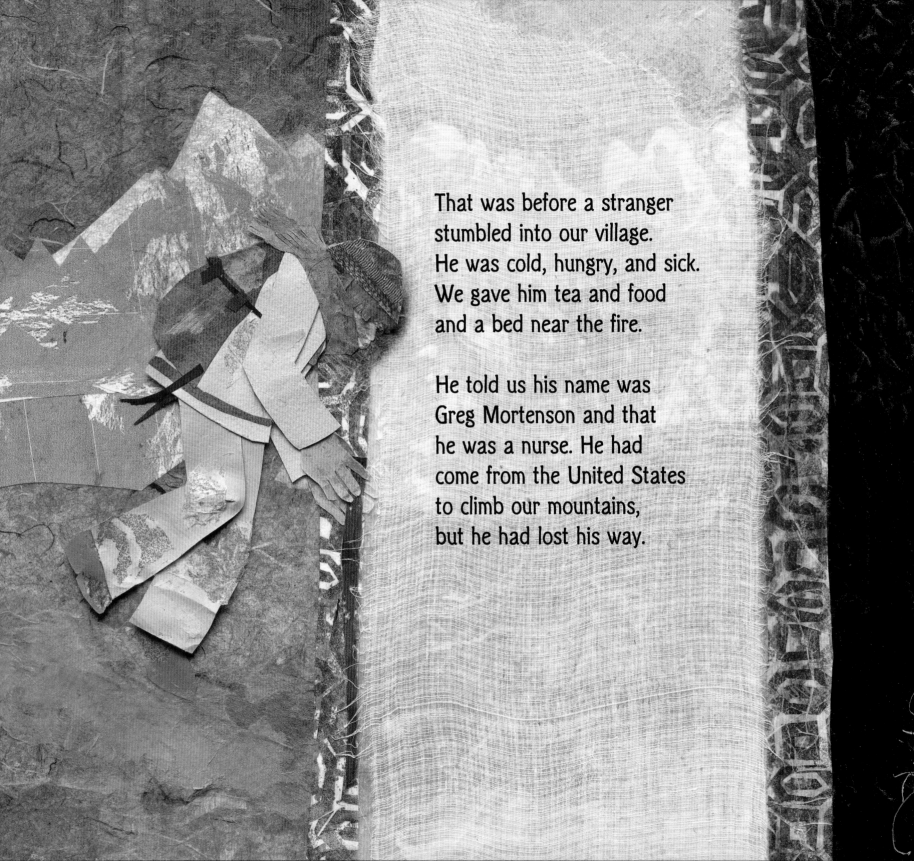

That was before a stranger
stumbled into our village.
He was cold, hungry, and sick.
We gave him tea and food
and a bed near the fire.

He told us his name was
Greg Mortenson and that
he was a nurse. He had
come from the United States
to climb our mountains,
but he had lost his way.

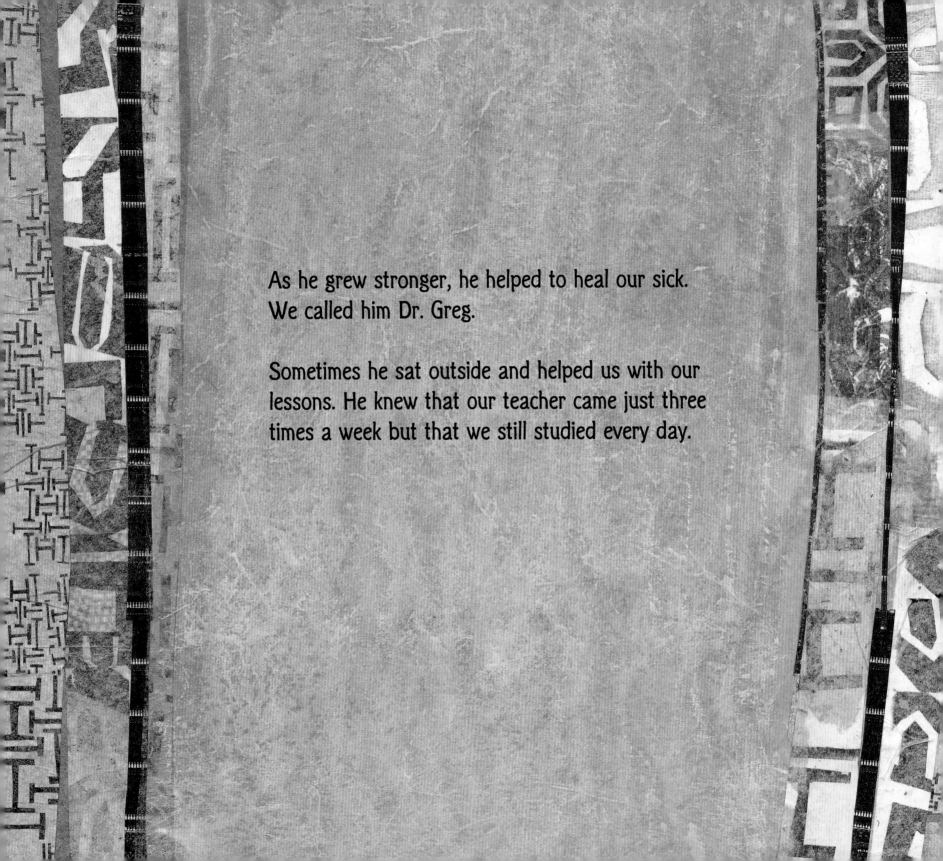

As he grew stronger, he helped to heal our sick.
We called him Dr. Greg.

Sometimes he sat outside and helped us with our
lessons. He knew that our teacher came just three
times a week but that we still studied every day.

When Dr. Greg was well enough to go
home, he asked Haji Ali, our wisest man,
to help him think of something special
he could do for Korphe.

Haji Ali answered Dr. Greg with a puzzle.
"LISTEN TO THE WIND," he said.

Dr. Greg closed his eyes.
From above the village on the high,
flat ground where we sat at our lessons,
the wind carried our voices down the path.
Dr. Greg heard our voices.
He felt the wind blow cold against
his face, and he understood.

Korphe needed a school.
Dr. Greg promised to come back
and help us build one.

We watched him walk
away until he disappeared into
the folds of the mountains.

One year later,
we saw a man walking on the
path far below our village.
It was Dr. Greg!
We all ran down to meet him.

In Skardu, the nearest big
town, he had collected the
lumber, cement, and tools that
we would need to build our
school. But, high above the
Braldu River, we had only a
single cable with a small box
that could carry a person
to our mountain from the next
one. There was no bridge.
Without a bridge, no one could
bring the heavy loads of
building supplies to Korphe.

So everyone worked together
to build a bridge from
our mountain all the way
to the mountain on the
other side of the river.

Many months later,
Dr. Greg and our fathers
and friends crossed the
strong, new bridge carrying
the supplies we needed to
build our school.

They continued to climb
until they reached the
place where we had piled
a mountain of stones,
cut from our own
mountains.

Haji Ali marked the exact spot
where our school was to stand.
Our mothers carried water to
mix the cement.
The men began to lay the
stones for our classroom walls.

With our small fingers we
wedged tiny slivers of stones
into the cement to make the
walls stronger. Our school
grew each day, up from the
high, flat ground where we
used to write with our sticks.

Finally the men attached the roof.
They asked Dr. Greg to hammer
in the last nail.
Our school was finished!
It was time to celebrate.

Our Imam, Sher Takhi,
our wise man, Haji Ali,
our teacher, Hussein,
Dr. Greg, who kept his promise,
Julia, the librarian who
brought our books,
the craftsmen,
the workmen,
the porters,
the grown-ups of Korphe,
the children of Korphe,
and even the yaks
and the dzos
and the goats
and the sheep
all marched together
to our new school.

Sher Takhi blessed the building.

We ran into our school with Hussein,
who now would come to teach us every day.

We are the children of Korphe.
We live in a village in the
mountains of Pakistan.
We write in Urdu
and English.
We add and subtract.
We read our books and
explore our maps.
We are learning in the school
that we helped to build.

We are the children of Korphe.
Can you hear our voices?

Listen to the wind . . .

A KORPHE SCRAPBOOK

This book tells a true story.
Greg Mortenson is a real person,

and the children of Korphe are real too.

Pakistan is a country in Asia,

and Baltistan is a region in Pakistan.
Korphe is a little village in Baltistan.

The mountains around Korphe are part of the Karakorum Mountain range.

This is Haji Ali, the wise man who told Greg to "listen to the wind."

Here is the bridge that was built across the Braldu River. It is 284 feet across and 60 feet above the water.

The Korphe men carried heavy supplies eighteen miles to the building site. The man in the very front of this line is Sher Takhi, the village prayer leader and spiritual guide, or imam. Carrying supplies was a very special gesture from Sher Takhi, because traditional Balti imams do not take part in physical tasks.

This is a picture of some of the men and children working on the walls of the Korphe school,

and here is the finished Korphe school, seen from the back.

Dr. Greg helped to cook the feast for the school's opening day celebration on December 10, 1996.

Then librarian Julia Bergman helped Korphe's teacher, Hussein, create a library for the school.

The Korphe school was the first one Dr. Greg helped to build. Since then he has overseen 131 more schools built in Pakistan and Afghanistan, such as this one in Hushe. Julia Bergman has helped to fill them with books. Teachers have been trained, and today nearly 58,000 children—more than 40,000 of them girls—attend these schools.

Children from all over the world help by collecting and donating pennies. A penny in the United States doesn't even buy a piece of gum, but in Pakistan and Afghanistan, one penny buys a pencil, and one dollar funds one child's education for a whole month. If you would like to help build schools with your pennies, contact Pennies for Peace at www.penniesforpeace.org.

Building schools requires lots of help. Each community helps with planning, materials, and labor. The Central Asia Institute, a group started by Dr. Greg and Dr. Jean Hoerni, helps with organization and funding.

My collage of Baltistan's apricot trees

Sharing fruit at the height of apricot season

My friend Julia Bergman described her first trip to Baltistan in colors:

> *"The stone and ice mountains are a monochromatic gray and white, and so are the clouds and the fog and the mist. But below the tree line is dense, green foliage full of apricots in every shade of orange in the world.*
>
> *"There are twenty-four varieties of apricots that grow in these high valleys. The people of Baltistan practically live on apricots. They eat them fresh, they eat them dry, they eat the inner kernels of the pits, and they make toys and jewelry from the outer parts. Nothing goes to waste in Baltistan."*

It was this vision of apricots that made me desperate to begin this project.

To help with my research, Julia sent me actual artifacts from Baltistan. These included fragments of ancient Buddhist architectural wooden carvings (some of which are preserved in Balti architecture), Balti talismans called *tomars*, traditional bird sculptures, and a Balti woman's typical hat.

The hat itself is like a sculpture of cloth fragments, bright colored yarn, and metal accents. I kept the hat on my desk for inspiration. One morning something glinted in the sun. Was it a square of metal? A bit of jewelry? I turned on my desk lamp and looked again. It was a *computer chip*!

Buddhist carving

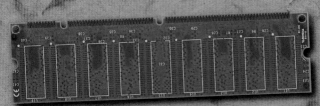
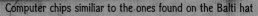

Computer chips similiar to the ones found on the Balti hat

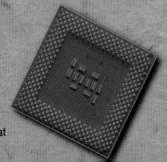

I studied the hat more carefully. What were the ridges of metal chain-like edgings that delineated the brim, top, and bottom? Halves of zippers, it turned out. The source of these items? Debris left by Western tourists. Julia was right: nothing goes to waste in Baltistan. It was moving to witness the deliberate, aesthetic use of things we would normally discard, and to realize that the women of Korphe share the collage medium with me.

Usually I buy heavy, expensive white paper on which to mount my work. I make a ritual of cutting my fine papers before beginning my illustrations. But this time I felt a bond with the resourcefulness of the hat-maker. This time, out of appreciation for her art, I felt compelled to piece my papers together with various scraps from my studio. I used tape and staples to make the base papers large enough. I made do with my own "found" materials.

As always, not one of these base papers is visible in the finished illustrations. But I like knowing that underneath every collage in this book lies another one. For me, these hidden collages reach across the world to my fellow artists, connecting me to the faraway friends I one day hope to meet.—S.L.R

Tomar

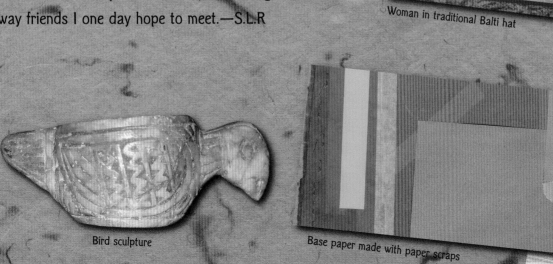
Woman in traditional Balti hat

Bird sculpture

Base paper made with paper scraps

ACKNOWLEDGMENTS
AAAHL, JR
Julia Bergman
Sharon Cresswell
Jeff Cymet
Nancy Feresten
Gamma One Conversions, Inc.
Lauri Hornik
Abdul Jabbar
Abdul Khaliq
Teresa Kietlinski
Uma Krishnaswami
Lily Malcom
Greg Mortenson
Alisha Niehaus
Nancy Patz
Ruth Phang
Jill Tarlau

Special thanks to the Pearson Foundation (www.pearsonfoundation.org) for sending an edition of this book in Urdu, the national language of Pakistan, to all the CAI schools.

BIBLIOGRAPHY

Three Cups of Tea: One Man's Mission to Promote Peace . . . Once School at a Time by Greg Mortenson and David Oliver Relin, Viking-Penguin, NY 2006

Pakistan, Faces and Places by M. Hanif Raza Colorpix, Islamabad, Pakistan, 1997

Mountains of Pakistan: Where Hell & Heaven Meet by M. Hanif Raza Colorpix, Islamabad, Pakistan, 1994

Baltistan in History by Banat Gul Afridi Emjay Books International, Peshawar, Pakistan, 1988

National Geographic: "High Road to Hunza" by John McCarry, photographs by Jonathan Blair p.114 March, 1994

National Geographic: "Baltistan: Twentieth Century Shangri-la" by Galen Rowell, photographs by the author and Barbara Cushman Rowell p.526 October, 1987

DIAL BOOKS FOR YOUNG READERS

A division of Penguin Young Readers Group • Published by The Penguin Group • Penguin Group (USA) Inc., 375 Hudson Street, New York, NY 10014, U.S.A. • Penguin Group (Canada), 90 Eglinton Avenue East, Suite 700, Toronto, Ontario, Canada M4P 2Y3 (a division of Pearson Penguin Canada Inc.) • Penguin Books Ltd, 80 Strand, London WC2R 0RL, England • Penguin Ireland, 25 St. Stephen's Green, Dublin 2, Ireland (a division of Penguin Books Ltd) • Penguin Group (Australia), 250 Camberwell Road, Camberwell, Victoria 3124, Australia (a division of Pearson Australia Group Pty Ltd) • Penguin Books India Pvt Ltd, 11 Community Centre, Panchsheel Park, New Delhi - 110 017, India • Penguin Group (NZ), 67 Apollo Drive, Rosedale, North Shore 0632, New Zealand (a division of Pearson New Zealand Ltd) • Penguin Books (South Africa) (Pty) Ltd, 24 Sturdee Avenue, Rosebank, Johannesburg 2196, South Africa • Penguin Books Ltd, Registered Offices: 80 Strand, London WC2R 0RL, England

Text copyright © 2009 by Greg Mortenson and Susan L. Roth
Collages copyright © 2009 by Susan L. Roth
All photographs © by Greg Mortenson unless otherwise credited
All rights reserved
The publisher does not have any control over and does not assume any responsibility for author or third-party websites or their content.
Text set in Clichee
Designed by Teresa Dikun
Printed in the U.S.A. on acid-free paper
10 9

Library of Congress Cataloging-in-Publication Data
Mortenson, Greg.
Listen to the wind : the story of Dr. Greg and Three Cups of Tea / by Greg Mortenson and Susan L. Roth ; collages by Susan L. Roth.
  p. cm.
Includes bibliographical references.
ISBN 978-0-8037-3058-8
1. Rural schools—Pakistan—Juvenile literature. I. Roth, Susan L.
II. Title.
LC5148.P18M67 2009   371.0095491—dc22   2008012268